Bridging the Gap: A Journey from

ENDORSEMENTS

BRIDGING THE GAP: A JOURNEY FROM LAW TO GRACE is a historical Biblical timeline that challenges the reader to take a closer intentional look at the plan of God for mankind through the conduit of the Hebrew people. It helps to clarify the importance of God's law given and the grace offered through His redemptive plan through the lives of the Hebrew nation. Bridging the Gap outlines the essential elements that existed before the Law, during the giving of the Law and understanding the importance of the Feasts, Holy Days and Sabbaths that remain applicable today in the purview of God's grace.

Minister Darius West, Teacher, Film Director
Los Angeles, Ca.

Bridging the Gap: A Journey from Law to Grace is 'Fresh Manna' for Believers! Apostle JR Armstrong brings to our understanding the revelation of Torah principles to those of us walking in 'Christian Darkness.' Darkness in the form of having zeal, but not according to knowledge. This revelation has both the depth and wisdom to lead new and old converts to a Greater Glory! This teaching is 'Kingdom made Flesh.' Finally, something we can understand…. something from God that 'Bridges the Gap! A true journey. Worth reading alongside the Word!

Steven G. Conley, Pastor
The Shepherd's Fold Ministries
Oklahoma City, OK.

Bridging The Gap
A Journey from Law to Grace

The author of this spiritual, literary piece, J.R. Armstrong has served in several ministries i.e., pastoral, evangelical, administration and teaching. However, Teacher J.R. as he is known thrives in theological research. In his new book, "Bridging the Gap-A journey from Law to Grace" he has 'out-done' himself in research. In addition, the book is eloquently written.
Most people, as they begin their spiritual journey, experience difficulty understanding and balancing the difference between the Old Testament Law and the New Testament Grace and how they should reconcile the two. Many Bible readers never get a clear understanding. Just as his title states, Teacher J.R. bridges that gap. This book is a 'must-read' for anyone who struggles with these truths.

Dr. Clarence Johnson, PhD
Senior Pastor
Transformation Church International, Inc.
Oklahoma City, Oklahoma

Bridging the Gap: A Journey from Law to Grace

SPECIAL THANKS

I dedicate this book and give all honors to Dr. Myles Munroe, my mentor, my inspiration, and my teacher. It's hard for me to cite everything he said because his teachings have become so intrinsically a part of me, Sometimes its difficult to disinguish his words from my thoughts.

I would not be the teacher I am today if not for Dr. Myles Munroe. Much of what I've written here is a culmination of my Hebrew studies and the Kingdom Principals I learned from Dr. Myles Munroe – some are direct quotes and some harvested from his many books.

I am also grateful to Rabbi Green for inviting me to attend Temple Isra'el for Hebrew Adult Continuation Studies, and getting me accustomed to the school. To Rabbi Sherman who was very patient and spent time with me after classes, and all the other instructors there.

In 1989, at the Azusa Conference, hosted by Higher Dimensions, led by Bishop Carlton Pearson, in Tulsa, OK – Dr. Myles Munroe birthed the teacher that I was impregnated with.

****

In 1984 the Holy Spirit had spoken to me while I was singing in the choir at Higher Dimensions. I continuously heard a voice telling me to write what I was hearing preached; then the same voice asked/commanded, *"Is that My Word? Study IT!"*; *"Write that down, did I say that? Study IT!"*; *"Write that down, is that what I meant? Study IT!"*

All the while I'm being flooded with images, thoughts, insights, and revelations of the Word like I never had before.

I said, Lord what are you telling me? Are they false teachers? He said, *NO! This is not an indictment on them. But I have called you to teach.* I said, Lord how will I become a teacher? Who's going to listen to me? The Lord responded – *"Before you can teach, you must first learn"*

Now, it took me a while to understand this was not an indictment on anyone who was speaking! I came to understand – THIS WAS FOR MY LEARNING! And what I learned was a yearning for the Word, as my understanding was increased. Through much prayer and supplication, I developed a thirst and a hunger for more of Him (the Word).

I sung in the choir for two years, and then the Holy Spirit told me to leave the choir and submit myself to the youth minister Pastor Thomas Brown. The youth ministry was an ever-increasing and powerful ministry at Higher Dimensions. After about two years there, I started attending Hebrew School at Temple Israel in Tulsa, Ok. Soon after, started having bible studies in my home under the banner of "Renewing the Spirit of Your Mind"

Bridging the Gap: A Journey from Law to Grace

It was during this time when I met Dr. Myles Monroe at the 1990 Azusa Conference. He chose me out of the crowd, as I worked with the usher ministry during the conference. He laid hands on me and said one word, "TEACHER" and I went out in the Spirit.

From that time until he went home, I was connected to him by email, newsletters, feedback, advice and spiritually. My life was never the same after that encounter at Azusa – I was pregnant with the Gift of Teacher, but it was his laying on of hands (a mid-wife, of sorts) that birthed that which I carried.

And, I would like to thank Joseph Good, Messianic Rabbi of Hatikva Ministries, for his book ***"Rosh HaShanah and the Messianic Kingdom to Come"***

Teacher's Instructions

I strongly encourage you, if you are to reap all that this work has to offer you, not to just read this as another novel, but to have your bible, hi-lighter, and note pad handy and readily available while reading this book. Pray for insight, revelation and discernment as you study along. Don't rush the process that took many years to develop: along the way I, myself, had many, many questions, and still do! But as you connect the dots, you will begin to see the big picture – don't rush the process, God's desire is to illuminate His Word and exact His will in your life – Kingdom presence.

Bridging the Gap: A Journey from Law to Grace

CONTEXT

ENDORSEMENTS 1

SPECIAL THANKS 2

FORWARD 5

INTRODUCTION 6

SECTION 1 9

    Pre-Law:

    Tithing – Gen 14.20

    Circumcision – Gen 17.10

    Sacrifices Gen 15.9-11, (Gen3.21)

    Sabbath Day(s) Gen 2.2-3, Ex. 16. 4-5, 18, 22

SECTION 2 18

    Shadow: From Egypt to Sinai

    Wilderness Experience: Keeping of the Law

        "…I am not come to destroy the law, but to fulfill". Matt.5.17

SECTION 3 34

    Substance: From Passover to Pentecost

    A substance of things to come Col 2.17

    Having a substance of good things Heb. 10.1

SECTION 4 47

    Grace: How now shall we live?

SECTION 5 63

    Conclusion

Bridging the Gap: A Journey from Law to Grace

FORWARD

There is a gap between the OT and the NT

    Historically, a 400-year gap

Physically, 4 generations

    Mentally, it's hard sometimes to even

See (understand) how they fit together

    Spiritually, one is Law the other Grace

What could they have in common?

    Religiously, we've discarded Law & embraced Grace

But … Jesus said, "I've come not to destroy the Law but to fulfill it."

My question to those who has thrown the 'baby out with the bath water' is this:

How did Jesus fulfill the Law?

This is our quest! When we discover how Jesus fulfilled the Law we will then and only then begin ***Bridging the Gap***.

June 8, 2006

Bridging the Gap: A Journey from Law to Grace

INTRODUCTION

There is much "gospeling", misquoting, taking out of content and out right misuse of the Word of God in the Body of Christ these days. The Bible says that in the end times, knowledge will increase. Now, I know technology today is on a first-class trip in a Lear jet. But in the Church, our theology seems to have gotten caught in some type of aero-loop: we're moving, but not reaching any particular destination, we going around and round the same old tenets.

As a teacher, my goal is to encourage you to think. Thinking (REASONING & CHOICE) is one of the most unique characteristics God gave mankind. Did you know that your beliefs are based on your thinking? Consequently, people *believe wrong* because they *think wrong*!

"Let this mind be in you that is also in Christ" Phil.2.5. Most people feel that their mind and their brain are synonymous. They're not! Our mind is a channel within our being that we can't touch, point to, nor put our finger on. This is the avenue by which Spiritual things are spoken to us. This thing that is in our heads is called a brain it is the link between flesh and soul. Our mind, since we can't see it, touch it or feel it, is the link between Spiritual/Soulish realm.

<u>Your mind is to your Spirit as your brain is to your flesh</u>

Bridging the Gap: A Journey from Law to Grace

The Bible also says, "As a man thinks in his heart, so is he." Prov.23.7 so, here the Bible is telling us that thoughts can come from our heart. Is there a brain there? Undoubtedly no! Therefore, our thinking processes are not exclusive to our brain. Ralph Waldo Emerson once said, "A man is what he thinks about all day long." The question is: what is the source of the thinking, the brain or the heart? Norman Vincent Peale said, "Change your thoughts and you change your world." When you renew the Spirit of your MIND, your circumstances may not change, but I guarantee the way you *see* them will.

In the office of my calling as a Teacher, my mission is to direct the "mind" to the Word of God, to seek Truth and to know Truth when it is found. Your brain is like a computer: it can only put out or respond according to what is programmed. Once your "mind" embraces Truth, your brain can then be reprogrammed to operate as one with your "mind".

So, as we go on this journey from Law to Grace, I will be pulling on you to submit your thinking to the Word of God. Yea, even to the point of provoking you to lay down your traditions and old mind set - that has had you in bondage.

I'm not going to bore you with all the different aspects of the Law. True, we are not living our lives under or according to "Law". But we have a better covenant called "Grace". The "Law" was for the Hebrew people only! It was the "Law" that set them apart - that made them peculiar. It was through the "Law" that the Hebrew people were to reveal to the world God's love for mankind and His plan of redemption.

Yes, His plan of redemption is embodied in the "Law". The plan was in the area of the "Law" that GOD told them to rehearse every year: **THE FEAST DAYS**. There was 7 feasts days that GOD gave to them after Israel's deliverance from Pharaoh. These feast days are foundational to the "Law" that was later given. And the central focus and core of each Feast is the coming of the Messiah, and the work of the Messiah.

For this particular study we will journey through the 1st feast, PASSOVER! This will encompass the 2nd, 3rd, and 4th Feast as well. I believe we will better understand the work of Jesus when we see this feast day unfolded.

These are the 7 Feast days (HOLY DAYS) God gave to the children of Israel:

THE FEAST DAYS / HOLY DAYS / HIGH SABBATHS

1. Pesach / Passover — Aviv (Nisan) 14

2. Hag haMatzah / Unleavened Bread — Aviv (Nisan) 15-21

3. First fruits of the Barley Harvest — The Day after the Sabbath during Hag haMatzah

4. Shavuot / Feast of Weeks — 50 days after First fruits of Barley Harvest

5. Yom Teruah / Feast of Trumpets — Tishri 1 Rosh haShanah

6. Yom Kippur / The Atonement — Tishri 10

7. Sukkot / Feast of Tabernacles — Tishri 15-21

We actually see these Holy Days on many of our calendars but ignore them because we are not aware of their significant.

SECTION 1

PRE-LAW

A good measure of understanding what something is, is to develop a concept of what it is not. TITHING, SACRIFICES, CIRCUMCISION, and SABBATH were **not** given as part of the "Law", but actually pre-dated the "Law". There was not a court, a judge, nor a law that held Abram accountable for keeping these things. There was only God's instruction to a man who heard, believed, and obeyed. This is why Abraham is called the "Father of Faith".

Jesus dealt with the Pharisees and their misinterpretation of the "Law". Tithing, sacrifices, circumcision, nor Sabbath (except for one incident) was never in question. Although the Pharisees gave tithes to be seen of men, and used the tradition of sacrifices for profit, also they boasted of their circumcision as a badge of honor over Gentiles, and used the Sabbath as a day of ritual exercises.

TITHING

I've heard the question asked many times, 'Do we have to tithe in this day and age, being that Jesus didn't teach on tithing?' Some may be attempting to justify why they don't tithe, and some are legitimately seeking answers. Well, they are right in saying that Jesus didn't speak directly on the act of tithing.

Bridging the Gap: A Journey from Law to Grace

We first learn of Tithing from Abram. He gave to Melchizedek, King of Salem, a tenth of his increase. (Gen14.20) Let me say right here, without changing subjects, that I believe that Melchizedek was the pre-incarnate Christ. So, in essence, Abram gave a tithe just as we do today: in the Spirit and Name of Christ – Jesus. This act of Faith by Abram set an example for faithful believers even in the absence of "Law". We don't need a "law" telling us this is the right thing to do. For we know that ALL belongs to HIM, and as a citizen of the KINGDOM we give up all rights of owning anything. Everything in a kingdom belongs to the king! HE only ask that we give (or invest) 10%, into the Kingdom, allowing us to live off the 90%. HE could have asked for all our money forcing us to depend solely upon HIM. But HE gave us dominion and reasoning; therefore, giving us the ability to manage our assets and resources.

At this juncture, let me point out a common problem in the Church today. WE DON'T PAY TITHES! To pay something gives one entitlement. When you pay your car note, it gives you ownership. When you pay your rent or mortgage, again ownership. When you pay your bills, it gives you certain rights – entitlements. In the book of Malachi 3.10, GOD said to test Him – *'that if you would bring the tithe, He would open the windows of heaven, and pour you out a blessing'*. Notice, He didn't say: If you pay your tithes and this is what you will get for your money… He said to bring it, which is an act of obedience on your part. This is not a commandment, it's a solemn promise that is contingent on your obedience. I Sam.15.22 says … *to obey is better than sacrifice* … Selah

Today, tithes are "paid', by church folk, as a responsibility and obligation to the church. Sometimes, our obligations and responsibilities are obliged grudgingly, just like we pay for our mortgage, car payment, child support, etc., but once completed we want credit or expect something specific in return. When Christians pay their tithes, at the end of the year they want a record of their giving so they can get a credit or write off on their taxes. Matthew 6:2 says, "…they have received their reward in full."

The Pharisees had developed that "pay" attitude which said they were entitled to be honored, to be blessed, and to be called holy: see the Parable of the Pharisee and the Tax Collector. (Luke. 18: 9-14).

OK, I'll say it again. **_WE DON'T PAY TITHES; WE SHOULD GIVE TITHES!_** Abram gave tithes to Melchizedek. This was pre-law. This was covenant era.

The very next chapter (Gen.15), we read of the establishment of the covenant GOD made with Abram. These passages will take us into next pre-law phase of Sacrifices.

SACRIFICES

GOD makes Abram more promises concerning his heir coming from his own loins, and his offspring being as many as the stars in the sky. Abram believed GOD and GOD counted it to him as righteous. But Abram asked GOD how shall he know that this will be his legacy. This question may appear to some that Abram doubted at this point. Not so! This was a legitimate question because this was a promise that Abram could not walk out in faith and see the fulfillment of it. This promise spoke of futuristic manifestations, things that Abram would not see. His question, his concern, his inquiry initiated what we call a "contract". What followed became the contract or "covenant" we call the Old Testament.

Gen.15.9, GOD instructs Abram in what animals that he should gather: a heifer, a she goat, a ram, a turtledove, and a pigeon. Five (5) animals (the number of Grace) all three (3) years old; the same age of the Passover Lamb in Egypt (to be discussed later); and the same age of Jesus' ministry.

Abram slaughtered the animals just as GOD had said and laid them on the ground, end to end. But GOD didn't show up right away. Consequently, Abram had to fight off the predators (buzzards) that smelled the fresh blood. In the Parable of the Sower: (Mark 4:4) the fowls of the air came to devour the seed that was sown. So, it was with Abram as it is with us today. Many times, we have to fight Satan to hold on to that which has been promised or we have to hold, by faith, that which we've already received in order to get that which is to come.

Abram fought the birds all day until sunset. Suddenly, a smoking furnace appeared over the slaughtered animals and what appeared to be a "burning lamp" walking between the sacrificial pieces.

Just as GOD had revealed to Moses (Ex. 32:20) that man could not stand face to face in the presence of GOD, man needed a substitute to make this covenant valid. The pre-incarnated Christ, the Anointed One stood in the gap, as a "burning lamp", *for man*, in the making of the original Old Covenant just as HE would do on the Cross, as Christ incarnate, the Passover Lamb, to establish the New Covenant.

CIRCUMCISION

In chapter 16, Sarai urges Abram to go into her handmaiden. GOD had promised a child and yet she was barren, therefore, Hagar would become a surrogate for them. But it didn't turn out that simple. Abram complied to Sarai's advice and Hagar looked down on Sarai after she realized that she was pregnant. Sarai evicted Hagar from the camp. While in the wilderness GOD

Bridging the Gap: A Journey from Law to Grace

heard her cry and sent her back. Meanwhile, GOD spoke to Abram concerning his heirs. Ishmael, Hagar's son would be blessed by GOD and greatly increased, but the covenant son would come from Sarai and his name would be Isaac. In fact, GOD changed both Abram and Sarai names to Abraham and Sarah, meaning father of nations and mother of nations.

At this point, can you imagine what Abraham is going through? NO, I don't suppose you can! Even with this great cloud of witnesses we have throughout the scriptures, GOD could speak the simplest command to us, like, "Go visit the shut-in", and we would have to pray about it first! SO, NO! I don't suppose we could understand what a man like Abraham was going through: Pioneering this faith movement without criteria, without any guidelines, without a mentor, without a pastor, nor a prophet. Only a voice – a compelling urge – a sense of power to accomplish everything asked of him. (We've read the story, after GOD gives him a son, GOD will ask for him back in a sacrificial act.)

But for now, GOD is about to establish another aspect of the covenant: The "sign" – or the signing, if you will, or the signature on the covenant. GOD goes over the covenant once again, (Gen. 17.2-9), promising that it will cover also his children many generations down the line. GOD is obligated and able to keep His side of the covenant. HE tells Abraham in vs10 that this is the part of the covenant you shall keep: every man child among you shall be circumcised.

So, this circumcision was the "sign" or "signing" of the covenant by Abraham. Every contract must have signatures to be valid. In vs13 ... *"and my covenant shall be in your flesh for an everlasting covenant."* And in vs14 ... *"whosoever is not circumcised, that soul shall be cut off from his people; he has broken my covenant."*

Abraham's willingness to accomplish the circumcision was in effect his signature!

Bridging the Gap: A Journey from Law to Grace

SABBATH DAYS

Genesis 2:2-3

"And on the seventh day God ended His work which he had made; and he rested on the seventh day from all His work which he had made. And God blessed the seventh day, and sanctified it: because that in it He had rested from all His work which God created and made."

There has been much controversy concerning the Sabbath Day(s). Questions such as: is the Sabbath still relevant for us today and, if so, which day should we keep – Saturday or Sunday? My humble opinion is that it is very relevant for us –on a spiritual level (meaning: what God purposed in it) and to recognize the significance of the actual day. God established the 7th day which is Saturday. He has not changed it!

Did Adam and Eve keep the Sabbath Day? The word doesn't mention any reference that they did, nor did Noah, Abraham, Isaac, Jacob or his sons.

After Jacob, whom God called Israel: his sons who are called Israelites, were deliverance from Egypt, God gave the tribes of Israel (his sons) the commandments, statues and law by Moses, commanding them to remember the Sabbath and keep it holy. These Commandments are also moral standards - which men ought to live by: the first 1-4 are reflective of our relationship with the creator, God; the 6-10 are reflective of our relationship with each other; the 5th one, right in the middle, (the number of Grace) is the commandment to observe the Sabbath day. Now, if we know and recognize the moral rightness in not stealing; not having other gods before the Creator, etc., (and these are relevant for us today) why is it so easy to disregard the 5th

commandment to remember the Sabbath Day and keep it holy? We want to change it to a time that fits our lifestyle and tradition – *forsaking the commandment of God* (Mark 7:8).

I am not promoting worship on Saturdays. In fact, on this side of the cross we are allowed to worship God any day of the week we desire, because we have a more excellent covenant. Our society traditionally worships on Sundays. But let's be clear – Sunday is not Sabbath Day of the LORD!

Colossian 2:16-17 says, *Let no man therefore judge you in meat, or in drink, or in respect of a holyday, or of the new moon, or of the Sabbath days: Which are a shadow of things to come; but the body is of Christ.* (Notice: Sabbath Days are plural, which I will explain later)

It was in the midst of their deliverance, while yet in the wilderness, God began to implement the practice of observing the Sabbath. *Then said the LORD unto Moses, Behold, I will rain bread from heaven for you and the people shall go out and gather a certain rate every day, that I may prove them, whether they will walk in my law, or no. and it shall come to pass, that on the sixth day they shall prepare that which they bring in; and it shall be twice as much as they gather daily.* (Ex. 16:4-5)

And the people did according to what God had commanded each day, some gathering much (and having none left over); and some gathering less (and having no lack) vs 18. And it came to pass on the sixth day they gathered twice as much (vs 22). *And Moses said, this is that which the LORD hath said, tomorrow is the rest of the Holy Sabbath unto the LORD; bake that which ye will bake today.... And that which remaineth over lay up for you to be kept until morning* (vs23). Here God establishes that they should rest on the Sabbath Day – and what they gathered on Friday (the sixth day), would multiple and be enough

The Pharisees accused Jesus of breaking the Sabbath (Jesus and His disciples gathered corn on the Sabbath) and His response was, *"The Sabbath was made for man and not man for the Sabbath: Therefore, the Son of Man is Lord of the Sabbath."* Mark 2:27-28 now, this is a very profound statement… for on this journey we will see exactly **WHY** the Sabbath was made for man, and **WHY** the Son of Man is Lord of the Sabbath! And **WHY** God rested (spiritual metaphor), and **WHY** He sanctified it (set it apart, physically).

Of the four tenets, mentioned above, sacrifices became an intricate, intriguing and intrinsic part of the Law. Heb 9.19 *"For when Moses had spoken every precept to all the people according to the law. He took the blood of calves and goats, with water, and scarlet wool, and hyssop, and sprinkled both the Book, and all the People."*

Sacrifices became a way of life for the Hebrew people. But as we read in vs 9 of the same chapter, the sacrifices *"…was a figure for the time present, in which were offered both gifts and sacrifices, that could not make him that did the service perfect …"* It was only a shadow *"…imposed on them until the time of reformation"* vs10.

Reformation is the act of reforming! Or manifestation!

Reform means to: amend, redeem, revise, correct, improve, reclaim, make over, or regenerate. We speak of the reformation pointing to the 16th century with the establishing of the Protestant church. But Christ was the Great Reformer! He came to redeem, reclaim, and to restore the Kingdom of God on earth and to reinstate man back to his intended place of dominion.

SECTION 2

FROM EGYPT TO SINAI

In order to build a bridge, we must first establish a firm, deep rooted foundation. The depth of your foundation determines how high you can build. So, lets dig deep here so as to go as high as the Spirit will allow us.

Let's look at who we are actually examining here. We are examining the people of God, those whom God called HEBREWS. We've been discussing Abraham, who was the first Hebrew. But…. God didn't define what a Hebrew was, and it seems strange that Abraham didn't ask. Throughout the rest of the biblical accounts, we still don't know what it means to be a Hebrew until the exodus from Egypt.

Keep your finger on that period right there. We'll come back to Exodus, but first I must deal with something right here. This is an epiphany in our foundation. We must understand that God didn't create a new "race" of people! Did God change Abraham's skin color? Did God change the texture of his hair? Did God alter Abraham's facial features? The answer is an emphatic NO! God didn't change anything physical about Abraham. Here's where we go deeper: the Hebrews of the bible are not the totality of todays so-called Jews! The Jews of today are a "race of people", or should I say an "identifiable political entity". But God never established a new race of people nor a political party.

Allow me to side bar for a moment and speak a little on political parties: I was reading up on the differences and similarities of the Pharisees and the Sadducees, and I had a compelling thought. The Pharisees and the Sadducees remind me of our two political parties Democrats and Republicans.

Bridging the Gap: A Journey from Law to Grace

The Pharisees represent the Democrats. The text says the name Pharisee is associated with the idea of separation; meaning, the "separated ones". This reminds me of the democrats because of their logo, a donkey or Jackass; I never understood why they chose such a symbol. I'm not sure if this is a self-designation or a derogatory label given by their opponents. The Sadducees (Republicans) were an aristocratic priesthood controlled by wealth and power, who trace their roots back to the High Priest of Solomon - Zadokites.

The Pharisees adhered to the Law but also added oral traditions and other mundane tasks to the burden of people. This caused a rift with the Sadducees, who taught that the people should *only* observe those things written in the word and reject the tradition and ideas likes resurrection, angels, and demons. This is similar to the rift with our two parties: The Republicans are concerned with growth through economic power of the few, (thereby not giving hope to the masses) and the Democrats believe growth should come from within by incentives to the lower class to better themselves.

Because the Sadducees' focus was strictly on the Temple and the Torah (Law), and not the common people, in 70 A.D. their sect disappeared without a trace when the Romans destroyed Jerusalem and the Temple. With that being said, to apply that to my comparison, if there was a total destruction of our economic system, and everyone was suddenly destitute, and everyone in the same class, the ideas of the Republican Party would no longer be relevant......... Nevertheless, that does not make the Pharisees (or the Democrats) the good guys because they survived! The Pharisees imposed hardships and gross misinterpretations of God's Word (today that would be: abortion, same sex marriage, etc.) to the point that Jesus called them a "den of vipers" and identified their "father" as Satan. (Just a thought!).

Bridging the Gap: A Journey from Law to Grace

OK, I'm back. Let's continue…

Abraham came from the land Urr of the Chaldeans. His two off-springs, Isaac and Ishmael: Sarah being the mother of Isaac was the promised child spoken of by God; Ishmael, whose mother was Hagar, an Egyptian, evolved into the people we call Arabs (or middle Easterners) today. Because Ishmael was Abraham's blood God made him a great nation, but Ishmael is not called a Hebrew! Being a Hebrew is more than bloodline, its spiritual; it's lifestyle. Let's get back to our period, the exodus from Egypt, and I will attempt to show you what God did establish!

The Bible says in Exodus 12:37-38 that 600,000 men besides women and children left Egypt and also a mixed multitude of other people. What this is saying is that not only did the Israelites depart Egypt but also Egyptians maybe and/or other ethic people that were in Egypt from Europe, Babylon, Greece and Africa. At the time Egypt was known as the world trading post, caravans traveled many miles just to trade for Egyptian goods. Many of these people were in Egypt during the plagues. They witness the hand of God against the Egyptians and were more than ready to leave with these people, that God seemed to favor.

Then we read in the 18th chapter of Exodus that Jethro, Moses' father-in-law, came to meet Moses at Mt. Sinai. Now Jethro, the bible tells us, was a Priest of the Midanites – Ex.3:1. Here's more depth in our foundation: the Midanites of the bible are the Ethiopians of today. Selah.

The milestone is this: at Mt. Sinai we have the Israelites, Egyptians, other ethic people and now Ethiopians. Here at Mt. Sinai God begins to issue out His" Laws". I'm not speaking of the 10 Commandments, but more so. God commanded them on what to eat, how to kill it, how to cook it, and how to keep it fresh and clean (kosher). God spoke to them about their relationships with each other and with strangers. God told them how He wanted them to serve Him. He re-established His covenant made with Abraham, Isaac, and Jacob and what He expected from them in return. In other words, God touched every aspect of their lives – setting them apart – which is the definition of sanctified – the same definition can be applied to consecration – to be set apart.

So, God set them apart from what? From the rest of mankind! God gave them a "new way" of life, not a new race but a new "lifestyle" – and they all agreed by saying "yes to God", "yes we will obey" Every ethnic group there said "yes". It didn't matter where they were from; they were all the epitome of what God called a Hebrew to be. This, in fact, is the same thing that defines a "Christian" today: not one's color, nor ethic group, but saying 'yes' to God. Selah.

In these chapters we come to 'know' what is meant by being a Hebrew. Therefore, being a Hebrew has nothing to do with the color of one's skin, or who your mother or father may be, nor where you were born. Being a Hebrew means saying 'YES' to God and living your life His way.

So, a Hebrew was someone who trusted God – was submitted to God – and willing to carry out God's plan of redemption.

I made a statement earlier that the Jews of today are not the totality of Hebrews in the Bible: 1st of all, because the Jews of today are, looked upon and spoken about, as a race of people (by blood line) – God did not make a new race. 2nd, the Hebrews were God's chosen people from the lineage of Adam, not because they were better than anyone else, but they were chosen to do a work. Their work was to reveal to the world God's redemptive plan for mankind. That's what the Laws were about, that's what the sanctification was all about, and that's what all the rituals along

Bridging the Gap: A Journey from Law to Grace

with the Holy Days were all about — the coming of the Messiah. The Jewish religious leaders, like Adam, have abdicated their responsibility, given up their authority for a self-proclaimed Doctrine of Piety. The genuine Hebrew is one who is a Hebrew inwardly (Spiritually).
Romans 2: 28-29,

****

Now, let's backup. The Exodus from Egypt is our starting point on this journey. Let's explore the spiritual meanings or shadows of the Exodus events.

Let's start with Moses. After receiving instructions from God, he returns to Egypt, he is standing before Pharaoh with a request/demand from God. And what is that demand? Exodus 5:3 tells us that Moses' words were *let the people go on a three-day journey into the wilderness to serve their God'.* WOW! His statement to Pharaoh wasn't "let my people go free" as we have been led to believe. But God said "Let the people go on a three-day journey into the wilderness to worship the Lord their God" Now to Pharaoh this didn't make sense. He worshiped many gods; in fact, He was told he was a god; he knew not of their god. He thought it was a trick. It was not a trick as much as it was a divine plan by God to redeem His people from bondage! Pharaoh was soon to come to know of the Living God of Abraham, Isaac, and Jacob. (By the way, it was Jacob whose name was changed to Israel, and his 10 sons and two grandsons became the 12 tribes of Israel.) Well after the ten plagues fell upon Egypt because of Pharaoh's contempt for God, Pharaoh conceded to let them 'go do as you have asked' Ex. 12:31.

It's the last of the ten plagues that we must focus on because it is vitality important. Ex. 11:1, God says that he will bring one more plague upon Egypt, and then Pharaoh will surely *thrust you out altogether*. This plague is the death of the first born of every family in Egypt, man and beast. Exodus 12 begins a very important aspect of the Gospel. The Passover! We act as though there's "no good news" until the New Testament. The "good news" started in the Old Testament, but it was hidden. I asked God why is Your Word a mystery and why was the truth hid? He told me it was not hid *from* me but was hid *for* me! That if I seek, I will find. It's sad to say but most time we don't see or except the Old Testament as Gospel. The Passover contains decrees, laws, commandments and truths; though greatly ignored, they cannot be escaped.

Exodus 12:2 begins with God giving Israel a "new" calendar. *This month shall be the beginning of months to you and the first month of the year.* This is actually the month of Nisan, the 7th month on the civil calendar. So, God is saying this month, Nisan, which is the 7th month as you know it, shall be the 1st month from now on to you. Take note here: God didn't change the calendar for everyone, just Israel. From this point on Israel has two calendars: a worldly calendar and a spiritual calendar. From this point on also whenever God speaks of a day or particular month/day/time He's referring to the "new" calendar. God instructed Moses to tell all of Israel to get a three-year-old, unspotted lamb on the 10th day of the month (Nisan) and bring it into their house until the 14th day. So, they kept the lamb in the house for 4 days. Why? Ex. 12:4 explains that every household should have a lamb. But if a man does not have a lamb or possible cannot afford a lamb, that man should join his house with his neighbor's house, so that all will be before a lamb. In the meantime, and in between time, everyone in the household has an opportunity, a responsibility, and a right to inspect the lamb – that it is indeed without blemish and worthy!

On the 4th day, which is the 14th day of the month, the lamb is killed. Here is a real nugget – vs. 6 says *the whole assembly of Israel shall kill the lamb in the evening* (KJV). Some translations say *at the twilight*, the original text (Hebrew) says *between the evenings*. To properly

Bridging the Gap: A Journey from Law to Grace

understand the meaning of this phrase *between the evenings*, you must understand time in the biblical era. (See the clock) Here in the 20th century, we began a new day at 12 midnight, but in the biblical era a new day started at sunset, let's say 6pm., in six hours it would be 12 midnight – six more hours and we're at 6 am, sunrise. Another six hours will put us at 12 noon, now here's the key, from 12 noon to 3 pm is called first evening, and from 3 pm to 6 pm is called second evening – then it is night time and a new day.

THE CIVIL CALENDAR

1. Tishri (Ethanium)
2. Cheshvan (Bul)
3. Kislev
4. Tevet
5. Sh'vat
6. Adar
7. Nisan (Aviv)
8. Iyar (Zif)
9. Sivan
10. Tammuz
11. Av
12. Elul

THE RELIGIOUS CALENDAR

1. Nisan
2. Iyar (Zif)
3. Sivan
4. Tammuz
5. Av
6. Elul
7. Tishri (Ethanium)
8. Cheshvan (Bul)
9. Kislev
10. Tevet
11. Sh'vat
12. Adar

Biblical Clock

The Exodus of Israel   *Time of the Sacrifice*

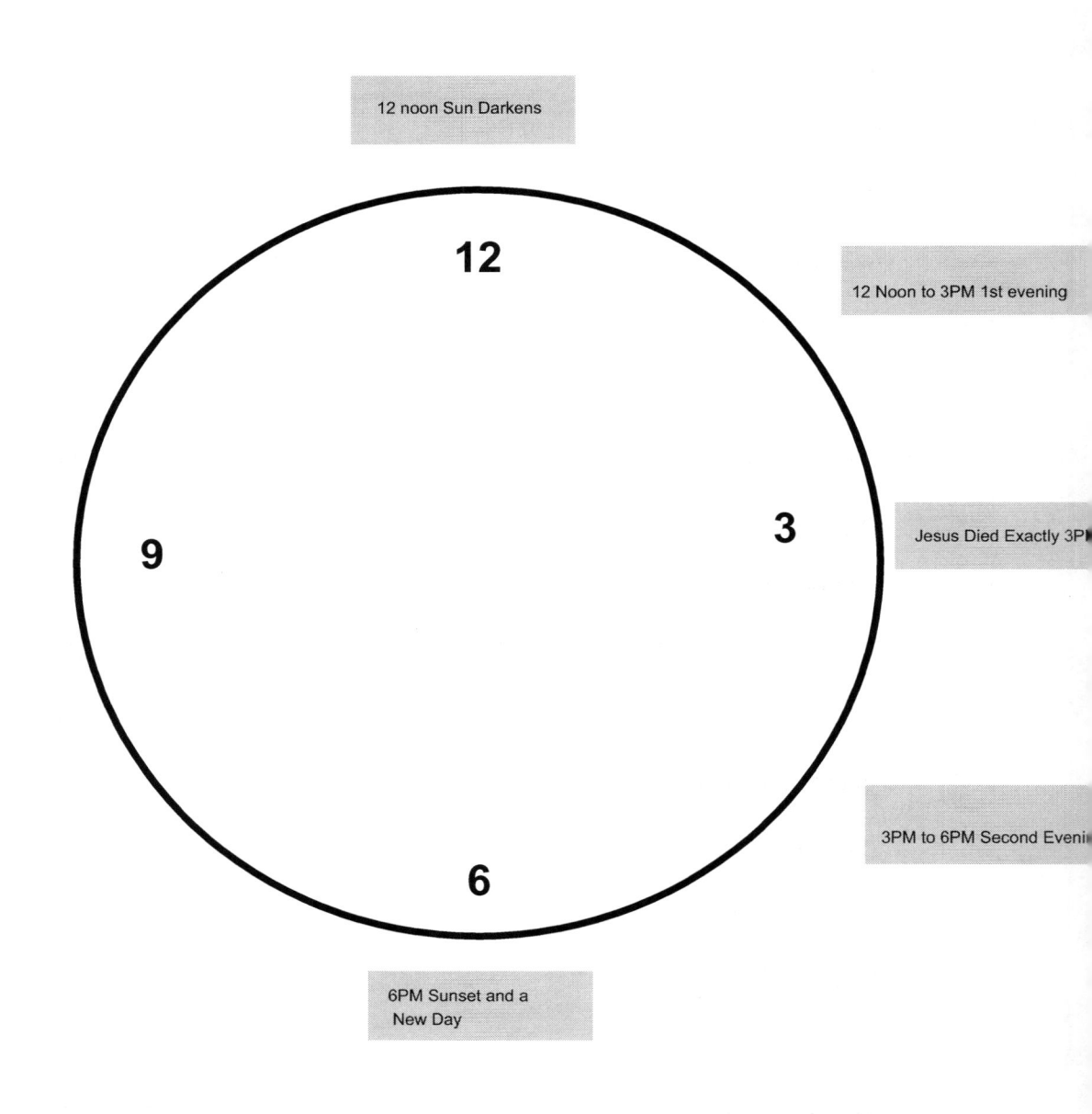

- 12 noon Sun Darkens
- 12 Noon to 3PM 1st evening
- Jesus Died Exactly 3PM
- 3PM to 6PM Second Evening
- 6PM Sunset and a New Day

Bridging the Gap: A Journey from Law to Grace

If you remember, Ex. 12:6 said for the whole congregation to kill the lamb *"between the evenings"*. That means every household was to kill the lamb all at the same time and at a specific time – **between the evenings.** What time was everyone to kill the lamb? (Look at the Clock)

At 3 pm! The lamb was to die once, for all, at the same time. God was very specific in His instructions because it forecasted a shadow of events yet to come.

They were then instructed to take the blood of the lamb and strike it on the door post of their houses, and cook the lamb by roasting it, not sodden, which means not to boil it. They didn't have ovens but open fire pits, so to roast the lamb it would have to be impelled on a rod and turned to completely cook it. They were to eat the meal with bitter herbs and unleavened bread. This imagery is so rich! Hind sight is 20/20, so looking back we can easily see this Passover lamb was a shadow of Jesus the Messiah. They were to eat it in haste for that night the Death Angel would kill every first born in the land of Egypt, except the houses where the blood was on the door post. It would be a sign of obedience and He would pass over that house with the death plague. That blood is still a sign today of those who are obedient to His word, it is the power of His blood that gives us redemption. It's the blood of Christ that covers us still that makes us appear righteous before God. Yes, I said appear to be righteous! Be not deceived, we are all guilty, but His blood renders us blameless.

Many do not associate the death of Christ with the exodus from Egypt. I encourage you to go back and read the 12 chapter of Exodus again, and I pray your eyes of understanding will be open to the awesome plan of God.

Moses goes and explains this whole plan of God to the people, and at the appointed time the plan unfolded just as God had said: at mid-night on the 14th of Nisan, every first born in

Bridging the Gap: A Journey from Law to Grace

every house in Egypt that did not have the blood of a lamb on the door post died- including Pharaoh's son. Now this is very significant as you will see later! The 31st verse of the chapter 12, Pharaoh calls Moses and Aaron told them to *"go and do as you have asked!"*

Verse 37 & 38 are milestones on our journey – Of the children of Israel, 600,000 men left Egypt, besides the women and their children, wow! But look at vs. 38 – and a mixed multitude also went with them! A mixed multitude means other ethnic people that were in Egypt at the time, from Europe, Babylon, Greece and Africa these are the same people I mentioned earlier. These are the people at Mt. Sinai who said "YES" to God.

Let me give you a little nugget right here that you can put in your back pocket, use it on a rainy day. In chapter 13:19, the first day of their 3-day journey, Moses goes and recovers the bones of Joseph. Joseph was a type and shadow of Christ – Moses went to Joseph's tomb to take him on their 3-day journey. Joseph being an anti-type of Christ, went on that 3-day journey and was submerged (symbolic of baptism) in the Red Sea. Therefore, when Jesus was crucified, he was placed in the tomb of a man named Joseph for 3 nights and 3 days. Selah!

Verse 20 is the 1st day of their journey; they journeyed from Succoth to Etham. Chapter 14:2, their 2nd day, they turned and traveled toward Pi-ha-hiroth, between Migdol and the sea. It was during this 2nd day that God hardens Pharaoh's heart causing him to go pursue the people and bring them back. When the people saw Pharaoh and his army, they were afraid and Moses speaks in the 13th verse a very prophetic statement, "Fear not, stand and **see** the **salvation** of the Lord…" this is the second time the word salvation is spoken in the Word (see Gen. 49:18). But it's the first time it's used as a demonstration and a prophetic manifestation. The power of God,

Bridging the Gap: A Journey from Law to Grace

parted the gulf (The Red Sea) that separated them from their deliverance and made a way where there seemed to be no way.

The work of the Cross, provided the same manifestation: there was a great gulf that separated mankind from God; Jesus stood in the gap, with one foot on the side of man and one foot on the side of redemption; saying don't charge it to them, Father - I'll take the burden – He bridged the gap for you and me.

Now, Moses stretches forth his staff and the waters of the Red Sea opens revealing a dry path for them to cross. How long would you imagine it would take for 600,000 men besides women and children, plus a mixed multitude to cross to the other side? Quite a while I would imagine. Meanwhile, God is holding Pharaoh and his army at bay until the right time. At the appointed time, God releases Pharaoh to pursue, and when they are all on the floor of the Red Sea, their chariot wheels began to fail (stuck in the mud) and God instructs Moses to return the waters to their natural state drowning Pharaoh and his army. Verses 24-27 tells us exactly the time of the day that this occurred, it was in the morning watch – *the next morning* – the 3rd day! The 3rd day they were FREE! God demonstrated the plan of **Salvation** in the events of the Passover.

Let's understand what is being said here. The children of Israel were considered Pharaoh's property. The law of the land of most civilized men says that when a man dies, his possessions will belong to his first born. Well, Pharaoh's son died in the 10th plague. There was not an heir to the throne, and God placed them (Hebrew's) so far from Egypt that even the succeeding Pharaoh could not (and probably would not) want to claim them, so they were free. Here's the principal, Moses ask Pharaoh to let the people of God go on a three days journey into

Bridging the Gap: A Journey from Law to Grace

the wilderness to worship God. The first day of their journey to them to Succoth (Exodus 12:13). Moses retrieved the bones of Joseph (Ex. 13:19), and the next day's journey took them from Succoth to Etham (Ex.13:20). Chapter 14, we find Pharaoh's heart is harden and he goes to bring the children of Israel back. When Israel saw the Egyptians, they were afraid and started murmuring. EX. 14:13 Moses tell the people to fear not. Stand still and see the salvation of the Lord. He raised his staff and the red Sea opened up for them to cross. Meanwhile, God placed a cloud between Israel and Egypt, Ex. 14:20. This cloud placed the Egyptians in total darkness but gave light to Israel for the entire night as they crossed the Red Sea.

When the cloud lifted. The Egyptians came, Moses lifted his rod again and the Sea closed in on the Egyptians, killing every one of them. Do you not understand what just happen? They went on a three-day journey: on the 3rd day they were on the other side of the red Sea; they are free. God's plan was perfect! God would not take a man's property arbitrarily, but when you defy Him, you may find yourself legally without those things you were so disobediently holding on to.

Let's look at other implications (shadows) of these events. This going down into the Red Sea and coming up on the other side free is symbolic of the later tradition of baptism; it also represents our understanding of being buried with Christ, as Paul spoke of, and as He (Christ) bored our sins, was crucified and buried in the earth 3-night and 3-days, yet rose, the 3rd day, that we all may be free from the penalty of sin; no longer enslaved to Pharaoh (Satan).

For the next leg of our journey, we must look back at Chapter 13 of Exodus as God establishes a memorial (Holy Day) with Israel. He tells them to remember this day that they were brought out of Egypt with a mighty hand. They were to mark that day, and sanctify to Him the

Bridging the Gap: A Journey from Law to Grace

first-born of man and beast as a yearly Holy Day. Then, in verse 6, God instructs further on how to memorialize it: the day after Passover, they are to eat unleavened bread for a week, and the last day of the week would be a great feast day. Leaven is synonymous to yeast, the ingredient that makes dough to rise. Yeast is to dough is, as sin is to our lives. Galatians 5:9 *"A little leaven leaveneth the whole lump."* A little yeast in your dough will cause your dough to rise into a loaf of bread. Therefore, sin in your life can cause your whole life to puff up with ugliness. Have you noticed; you can only keep bread for so long before it begins to mold? Sin will do your life the same way!

Therefore, beginning the day after Passover, the Hebrews would rid the house of all leaven, which means for us, too, to rid our lives of sin: it's a time of self-examination. Here we have two Feast Days or Holy Days, the Passover and the Feast of Unleavened Bread, established by God and verse 9 tells us that this is God's Law. (Exodus 13:9)

Now there two more feast days attached to these two feast days, and it is the Feast of First Fruits and the Feast of Pentecost. To explain these, we must go to Leviticus 23. In verses 1-3, God reiterates the weekly Sabbath (6 days of work and the 7th day is Holy). In verses 4-8, God again reiterates the two Feast Days (Passover and Unleavened Bread). In verse 9 God is now introducing a new Feast Day called the Feast of First Fruits. Verses 10 & 11 *"... when you come into the land, I will give you and you reap a harvest; you shall bring a sheaf of the first fruits to the priest. And he shall wave it before the Lord to be accepted for you on the morrow after the Sabbath (of Unleavened Bread).* When I was a youngster (child to teenager), I remember a song they sung in the Church of God in Christ: Bringing in the sheaves, bringing in the sheaves, I will come rejoicing bringing in the sheaves. I laugh at myself now because I sung with them but I always sanged "Bringing in the sheep" LOL. But hindsight is 20/20. I now see what they were singing about.

When we move to verse 15, we find God is giving them another feast: The Feast of Pentecost. *"And you shall count from the morrow after the Sabbath, from the day you brought the sheaf of the wave offering, seven Sabbaths. And the morrow after the seventh Sabbath shall be fifty days…"* I submit to you now that God is establishing Pentecost as a Feast, the shadow that was casted at Mt Sinai. I will explain later.

Let's deal with the Feast of First Fruit. The exact day of observance of First Fruit was been greatly debated by Pharisees and Sadducees and now by priest and Christians alike. The debate lies in the wording of the scripture in Lev. 23:11. I can't clear up the debate but maybe I can help you understand what the debate is about: not only did God establish Saturday (the last day of the week) as the Sabbath Day but the Feast Days were also called Sabbath Days, but more specifically, "High Sabbaths". So, the controversy is this; is the scripture referring to the weekly Sabbath (during the week of Unleavened Bread) or the High Sabbath (at the end of Unleavened Bread). Whichever one it's referring to; we do know that Jesus is the first fruit of the resurrected (1 Cor.15:20-23).

What happens at Mt. Sinai was a shadow of Pentecost that would manifest itself in Acts of the Apostles, Chapter 2. Now what happen in the days leading up to Pentecost? Luke, who is the writer of Acts of the Apostles, tells us in chapter 1:3 that Jesus spent 40 days with His disciples after His resurrection. Verse 4 Jesus commands them to remain in Jerusalem and wait for the promise of the Father. How long did they have to wait? 10 days! There's isn't a scripture to confirm this, but we can infer this summation because the prefix "Penta" means 5. Pentecost

Bridging the Gap: A Journey from Law to Grace

means 50, remember Leviticus 23: 15 – they were to count 7 Sabbaths (that's 7 weeks), and the next day was the Feast of Pentecost (7×7+ 1=50). In this case we're talking about 40 days that Jesus was seen by the disciples and how much longer until the Holy Ghost fell to establish the Feast of Pentecost? 10 days (40+10=50).

Acts of the Apostles, Chapter 2 begins, *"And when the day of Pentecost was fully come..."* In other words – here's the substance of the shadow that was given. Verses 2-4 tells us, there came from heaven as of a mighty rushing wind; and there appeared cloven tongues as of fire that sat upon each disciple; and they were filled with the Holy Ghost and began to speak in other tongues. Where's the shadow on Mt. Sinai? Let move to Exodus 16:1 the word tells us that they arrived at the Wilderness of Sin on the 15th day of the 2nd month after leaving Egypt. The Wilderness of Sin is a desert region. Exodus 19:1. The Word says in the 3rd month that they left Egypt; they came into the wilderness of Sinai and camped at the Mt Sinai. (Most scholars will attest that this journey from Egypt to Sinai took 50 days and coincides with the out pouring of the Holy Ghost at Pentecost, 50 days after Jesus' resurrection). This is when and where God began to implement His laws, His statues, and His commandments and to give them a life-style by which to live and to be identified by. Here for the first time, God revealed man's part in the covenant and what it is to be called His people - a Hebrew.

Leviticus 19:8 tells us that all the people answered YES; we will do all that the Lord has spoken. This day God consecrated them; set them apart from the world. He touched every aspect of their lives; He gave them a new life-style and they all said YES. It's their obedience that made them God's people. Just as our obedience that makes us Christians. Christian is not a nationality; neither is Hebrew; Christianity is not ethic; neither is Hebrew; and it's not one's creed or color of skin; neither is Hebrew: but he who says YES to God! Now remember, who are all the people there at Mt. Sinai? Well, over 600,000 Israelites besides there women and children, a mixed multitude of others and also Jethro, Moses' father-in-law, and his people the Midianites (who today are identified as Ethiopians). Everyone there adopted this new life-style. In verses 16-18 it's recorded, the voice of God was like lightning, and thundering, and fire descended from heaven on the mountain, and all the people heard, saw, and trembled. Whether everyone spoke one language is doubtful, but they all heard and understood in their own language or dialect. Is that not the picture of the events in Acts of the Apostles, the 2nd chapter, the Day of Pentecost?

Acts of the Apostles 2: 1-4, And when the Day of Pentecost was fully come, they were all with one accord in one place. Vs 2, And suddenly there came a sound from heaven as of a rushing mighty wind, and it filled all the house where they were sitting. Vs 3, and there appeared unto them cloven tongues as of fire, and it sat upon each of them. Vs 4, and they were filled with the Holy Ghost, and began to speak with other tongues, as the Spirit gave them utterance.

Bridging the Gap: A Journey from Law to Grace

SECTION 3

SUBSTANCE: Grace

Our journey so far has been interesting and revealing. The remainder will pull on your understanding of what's been revealed to you. It's going to require application. As in most applications, some old things must be removed so that the new can be laid properly.

With that said, let's move forward in time. Jesus, being 33 years old, has done many miracles: turning water to wine; giving sight to the blind; making the lame to walk; and raising the dead. In the book of St. John, the 12th chapter, we will pick up our story and continue our journey to discover more substances to the shadows we've examined already.

The first verse of John 12 is a key to letting us in on the plans and purposes of God. It is 6 days before Passover, and Jesus arrives in Bethany, where Lazarus lives, which is just outside of Jerusalem. Mary, Lazarus' sister anoints Jesus with some very expensive oil. Verse 12 tells us that the next day (5 days before Passover) Jesus went into the city of Jerusalem. There in the city the people were having a huge gala (Passover is their most highly celebrated time), the whole city is a buzz. Here the people lay down palm branches before Jesus to honor Him, as He enters the city riding a white ass. The rest of chapter 12 reveals Jesus' teaching as all manner of people gather to see and hear, including the Pharisees.

Let's stop and connect the dots here so that we can see where we're at. This is the week of Passover, so let's apply God's instructions: Four days before Passover the lamb is brought into the house. Now at this time in history, individuals are not bringing a lamb into their houses to sacrifice. The lambs, called temple lambs, are raised corporately by shepherds for the priest to sacrifice. On the 10th of Nisan, the priest goes out in to the fields to retrieve a lamb for the Passover tradition. When the priest enters the city with the sacrificial lamb the people sing 118 Psalms. He parades the lamb through the city for all to see and delivers the lamb to the temple, the House of God. Not long afterwards, Jesus would enter the city riding a white ass. The gaiety of the people: and with much wine, the music and dancing, sees Jesus, being paraded as it were, on a white ass, they went ahead of him laying palm branches and cried, *Hosanna, blessed is the King of Israel that cometh in the name of the Lord* (Jn. 12:13). Jesus would have gone into the temple to teach on this particular day, and people came to ask questions of Him, and as He is being examined, the sacrificial lamb was also in the temple under inspection. This is the 10th of Nisan! (Oh, did I not tell you? The reason the lamb is kept in the house for four days, is for the inspection: to assure it is without blemish or spot).

Chapter 13 opens, *"Now before the Passover…"*, so we are still within the four days. "…when Jesus knew that His hour had come that He should depart out of this world…" this day is most likely the day before Passover, and Jesus and His disciples have gathered for a last supper together. Mind you, this is not a Passover meal, but simply the last supper they will have before His crucifixion. This is the supper where Judas is revealed as the betrayer. **In his chapter Jesus washes the disciple's feet, and begins to pour out His heart like never before: he gives them a new commandment; he tells them of Peter's denial; about the power of the believers; the coming of the Comforter and the work of the Holy Spirit; the believers as branches and Himself as the true vine; that prayer as the key; about the Holy Spirit glorifying Christ; the**

Bridging the Gap: A Journey from Law to Grace

attitude of the world towards the disciples; that prayer as the source of joy; about the flock being scattered; Christ the great intercessor; the definition of eternal life; that they should pray for restoration; to prayer for the church; to pray for the keeping the saints; to pray that the church be kept pure; to pray for unity of the church; and the exaltation of the church. Jesus reiterated things He'd already told them and He told them everything they should know; He poured it out and poured it out; He emptied Himself in a most significant way.

Just imagine you've gathered your family together, and you know, even though they don't fully understand, it will be your last chance to reveal your heart before you die. This is how I perceive this few chapters (13-17), Jesus pouring out His heart to His family, His last chance to help them understand their future and what they are up against.

Chapter 18 opens as they leave the upper room to go to the Garden of Gethsemane. It is here under the pressure of obedience, (Gethsemane means oil press; a place that applied tremendous pressure to extract the precious oil from the olive), that Jesus laments as He steps into the next phase of His purpose. He leaves His disciples, except for 3 (Peter, James, and John), and goes deeper into the garden to pray. Along with the pressure, I'm sure frustration came because His trusted friends could not stay awake to pray with Him. It was most likely the combination of the pressure of the situation he was about to face; frustration with His friend and simply feeling alone that Jesus' flesh cried out "Father let this cup pass from me"! The pressure was so great at this point that the capillary blood vessels that feeds the sweat gland ruptures. This happens under conditions of extreme physical or emotional stress, indicating acute fear. Nothing

Bridging the Gap: A Journey from Law to Grace

we have ever faced will compare or exceed this Gethsemane experience. Nevertheless, Jesus said Not my will but thine will Father be done!

Judas arrives with the soldiers and they arrested Jesus and took Him to Annas' house before they presented Him to Caiaphas the High Priest, who was Annas' son. The priest had Him questioned, beaten, and humiliated before sending Him to Pilate. To keep you on track, read verse 28: Jesus was led into the Hall of Judgment to Pilate, but the Jews themselves did not go in lest they be defiled, because Passover was nearby. So, you see, here at this juncture, Jesus is being examined, under inspection and we are still within the four days; between the 10th and 14th of Nisan. Just as the sacrificial lamb is on display in the Temple, so is the Lamb of God before the world. Atlas, Pilate announces in verse 38, *I find in him no fault at all!* Alleluia! Alleluia! Worthy is the Lamb of God!

As we move to the 19th chapter, here we will find a very crucial and interesting stumbling block. Here is where I believe the "church" made the wrong turn, not discerning the signs. Verse 14 says, *"And it was the preparation of the Passover, and about the sixth hour: and he (Pilate) said to the Jews, Behold your King!"* This is crucial because we, "the church" know that the day of preparation is (Friday) the day before Sabbath (Saturday). But this was not the weekly Sabbath but a High Sabbath: every Feast Day is also a Sabbath Day; but to distinguish the Feast Day Sabbath from the weekly Sabbath, the Feast Day Sabbaths are call High Sabbaths. (John. 19:31), it was a High Day, it was Passover. NOT THE PREPARATION DAY OF FRIDAY FOR THE WEEKLY SABBATH. This is also crucial to understand, that, that week there were two preparation days and two Sabbath days. Why is this so crucial? Because, to understand the events that occurred the week Jesus was crucified, gives revelation that the tradition of Palm Sunday, Good Friday, and Easter are all not Biblically correct, and are actually based on pagan practices. We will cover this more in depth later.

Let us move now to Mark the 23 chapter and the 44th verse. Mark gives us a little more detail into the happenings about the sixth hour. Vs.44 *"And it was about the sixth hour, and there was darkness over the earth until the ninth hour."* Vs.45 *"And the sun was darkened, and the veil of the temple was rent (torn) in the midst."* V2.46 *"And Jesus cried with a loud voice, 'Father into thy hands I commend my spirit': and having said this, He gave up the ghost"* Mark is giving us 3 details that we can follow, dots that we can connect, to see the big picture.

We've already discussed and described time (pg. 23) and how time was applied to a typical day in the biblical era: each new day starts at 6pm. In addition, remember, when the Bible speaks of a particular hour of the day, it is referring to the DAY TIME hours. So, when you read the sixth hour, as there are several references in the Word, it is speaking of 12 noon, the sixth hour of DAY LIGHT, not when the day started. If it was the sixth hour of when the day started, it would be midnight: the sky cannot get dark at midnight, it's already dark. The night hours are "watches" 1st, 2nd, 3rd, and 4th watch – each watch is 3 hours long.

So, #1, Mark is telling us that Jesus was put on the cross at noon. And from noon to 3pm darkness fell upon the earth. #2, while the sun was darkened, at the 9th hour (3pm), the veil in the temple was rent, (and we understanding it was rent from the top down). Why is this important? Because it gives us an exact time that Jesus died. This is the exact same time the children of Israel were told to kill the lamb back in Egypt! WOW! For a greater understanding of the Word,

Bridging the Gap: A Journey from Law to Grace

we need to conceptualize the principals being shown to us. Jesus said the words I speak to you are spirit and life (Jn.6:63). The Old Testament is a shadow of the New Testament. The shadow is the spirit of the principal and if you follow the shadow, it will lead you to the life of the principal, which is CHRIST.

God placed us in time to give us a tool of measurement, but we are fallible. Everyone's not on the same time. Some people time is fast, some are slow and some have no since of timing at all. We have time zones. 3 o'clock in New York is 12 o'clock in California. God doesn't live in time as we do. He's outside of time; He's in control of time, He's not too fast, nor too slow, He is always on time. So, it should be no big surprise that His timing is precise.

God is eternal and in eternity time does not exist, as we know it. Let me give you an example: when Moses went to see the burning bush that was not being consumed, Exodus 3:5, God spoke to him, *"... put off thy shoes from off thy feet, for the place whereon thou standest is Holy ground."* Moses was standing in the presence of eternity! The bush did not and could not burn up because it takes time for anything to burn. Let everything be established by two witnesses. Witness #2 – the three Hebrew boys Shadrach, Meshach, and Abednego (Daniel 3:16-28), did not burn, because the fire had no power over them because there was a 4th person in the furnace with them *like the Son of God*. So, they too, were in the presence of eternity in which time ceased to exist.

Now, detail #3, Jesus was in total control of His life. He didn't wait for the Roman soldiers to come and break His legs before He died (Jn. 19:33), like the two thieves. Jesus laid

Bridging the Gap: A Journey from Law to Grace

down His own life at the appointed time. *"No man takes it from me, but I lay it down of myself..." Jn.10:18*

With those details behind us let's go back to John the 19th chapter, and pick up our journey in the 28th verse. Jesus was thirsty and they gave Him vinegar on hyssop. And when He had received it, *He said 'It is finished'*, and died. (This is a very interesting statement for Jesus to make. I believe these words of Jesus has been misinterpreted and misapplied. I will deal with that later). Now we already know that Jesus was in control of time. Why would He ask for something to drink when He's going to die in the next few moments? To fulfill scripture! Remember in Egypt, God told them to eat the lamb with bitter herbs? Hyssop is an herb and vinegar is bitter. So, he asked for drink and they gave Him bitterness. He received it as a substance to the shadow that was caste. This is salvation manifesto! Salvation is good but it's not sweet. Someone had to die! You, too, must die to your old self and become a new creature!

Jesus died to pay the price of redemption for us; So that we may once again have a right to the Tree of Life; Assess is free to us because of Jesus, but to obtain and maintain our salvation the old man must die and remain dead. So, there's a death that must come from within us; a sacrifice, a lying down of our own life, willingly just as Jesus did. Jesus said to take up your cross and follow me, and many attempts to simulate this with the troubles we face. But Jesus did not just carry the cross; He lay down on the cross; was nailed to it; and gave Himself to it.

These words of Jesus, "It is finished", are a very interesting thing to say at this particular time. I believe this statement "It is finished" have been misunderstood and misapplied by many. It has been said that Jesus meant just what He said, it is finished; all is complete, there's nothing left to do, my work is done, all these conjectures and others I've heard in my life time. The fact of the matter is that Jesus was speaking specifically about one thing, SALVATION: the sin debt!

Jesus' overall work was not complete yet; in fact, He's still at work today interceding on our behalf, and preparing a place for His bride, the Church. But before the interceding commenced, there was work Jesus yet had to perform. Remember, Jesus is the substance to the shadows that had eluded and mystified these people for generations. God gave them the institution of sacrifices in the Old Testament; the best offering being the unblemished lamb. Here's a Question: In all the stories of old, did a lamb ever come back to life; in other words, resurrected? The answer of course is NO! so what I'm saying is that, it was His death ONLY that was necessary for the redemption, to pay the sin debt: His resurrection represented something else. First of all, as King, He cannot rule and reign in His Kingdom from a grave. He had to rise up to receive His Kingdom and to set the standard of the citizens of that Kingdom.

Here we come to the stumbling block I spoke of, verse John 19:31: *"The Jews therefore, because it was the preparation, that the bodies should not remain upon the cross on Sabbath day,* **_(for that Sabbath day was a high day) ..."_**. re-read your bible again and see if your version says the same thing or something similar. IT WAS A HIGH SABBATH DAY! Meaning it was a Feast Day - NOT THE WEEKLY SABBATH OF SATURDAY! Here's how we stumbled, we know preparation day is the day before Sabbath, so we <u>assumed</u> this was Friday, the day before Saturday. We were wrong! That particular week there were two Sabbath days – Passover Sabbath and the weekly Sabbath. Jesus could not have been crucified on a Friday and rose on Sunday and still fulfill the scripture, Matthew 12:40, Jesu spoke of the Son of Man being in the heart of the earth **three days** and **three nights**. You do the math! Actually, He was crucified two days earlier, on Wednesday. This should seal the casket on the Easter myth!

PASSOVER WEEK
(JESUS CRUCIFIED)

Crucifixion			Wednesday @ 3:00pm Shofar is blown
			@ 6:00pm Celebration of Unleavened Bread
High Sabbath	1	*Thursday* (A)	Feast of Unleavened Observed
	2	*Friday*	Day of Preparation (Weekly Sabbath)
Resurrection	3	*Saturday*	Sabbath Observed (Resurrected @ 3:00pm)
		Sunday (B)	Feast of First Fruit (Wave Offering)
			Jesus Manifested Body (First Fruit of the resurrected)

A **Feast of Unleavened Bread**
Life out of the ground (Manna)
(Ex.16.4) (Det. 8.3, 16) (Jn.6.31-38)

Unless a grain falls and dies....
(Jn.12.24)

Jesus was **Planted** not Buried

B **Feast of First Fruit (Barley Harvest)**
The first pick of the Harvest is brought to the Temple

Jesus is the First Fruit
(1Cor.15.20)

Bridging the Gap: A Journey from Law to Grace

That particular year Jesus was crucified, Passover began Wednesday at sunset (6pm), Because the Feast Day approached, Joseph of Arimathea and Nicodemus asked for the body of Jesus, to lay Him to rest; for sunset was near. They had three hours to prep His body and get it in the tomb, because at sunset they could not do any work and had to be home themselves.

Well, they placed Him in the tomb; remember it was the day of preparation, the day before the High Sabbath Day (Passover), Wednesday. Passover takes them through Thursday. Friday is the day of preparation for the weekly Sabbath, on the Sabbath Day (Saturday), I believe, according to the Word, Jesus rose exactly at 3pm, just as He (Jesus) had proclaimed, (3 days and 3 nights). Early Sunday, the first day of the week, the women came to the tomb to dress Him properly for burial suited for their Messiah. But He was not there! The Angel told them *"He has risen"*, past tense, already done; the angel did not say, you just missed Him. Well, when did He rise? Jesus said Himself that he would be in the earth 3 days and 3 nights (Matt. 12:40) once again, I say, you do the math!

Well maybe the math does not convince you, the Word will testify of itself. Mark 2:23-28 is the story of Jesus and His disciples picking corn on the weekly Sabbath Day, and the Pharisees confronts them that is of unlawful to pick corn on the Sabbath Day. And Jesus says to them in vs. 27 & 28 *"... man was not made for the Sabbath but the Sabbath for man. Therefore, the Son of Man is Lord also of the Sabbath"* Wow, what a profound statement! The Sabbath was established for Him, for His resurrection, it is His day, His day of rest! Remember on the 7th day God rested from all he had created, he blessed it and sanctified it. He (God) set it (Saturday, the weekly Sabbath) apart from the other days. This has such profound meaning. If we would go to

Bridging the Gap: A Journey from Law to Grace

the book of Colossians 2: 16-17, the word tells us that the Sabbaths Days are a shadow of things to come, and that they would be centered in Christ. It is also testified in Hebrews 4: 1-9, where the Sabbath is spoken of in three ways: (1) as the literal weekly rest, (2) as the rest that is to be had by faith in Christ, and (3) as the seventh day of rest yet to come, a prophetic day in the Lord. So, the Sabbath is not a just a day to go to church, to worship, to give to Him; but the Sabbath was created, blessed and sanctified for the rest we can attain in Christ and we obtained it by the resurrection, as He established it.

Yet, the work was not finished, let's go to the book of John, the 20th chapter 1st verse tells us that early, while it was still dark, Mary went to the tomb and found the stone had been rolled away. Weeping because she thought someone had stolen the body; saw a man she perceived as the gardener. But when He spoke her name (vs 16), she recognized His voice and responded "Rabboni" which means Master. Now, here is another nugget, verse 17, *"Jesus saith to her, Touch me not: for I am not yet ascended to my father: but go to my brethren, and say to them. I ascend unto my Father, and your Father, and my God, and your God.*

Verse 19 tells us that *"the same day, at evening, being the first day of the week...came Jesus and stood in the midst and saith unto them. Peace be unto you."* He showed the disciples His hands where the nails went through; He showed them His side where he was pierce by the spear.

Now, this is crucial, why could Mary not touch Him but a few hours later the disciples could? Christ had to finish the work of the High Priest! If I may, again, remind you of an Old Testament shadow of the High Priest: once a year, on the Day of Atonement, the High Priest would take the blood of the lamb into the Holy of Holies, behind the veil where God dwelt with them in that dispensation. Once behind the veil, the High Priest would sprinkle the blood of the lamb on the mercy seat before the presence of God for atonement for the sins of all the people. There was only one High Priest and ONLY he could perform this task. The High Priest had been consecrated for this; he had on special garments for this task; once the High Priest had begun this ritual, he could not be interfered with, touched, or allowed anything to defile him.

Remember, when God instructed Moses to build the tabernacle and the Holy Place: He told Moses the length, width, and the height of the tabernacle; God told Moses what kind of wood to use in each section and which wood should be overlaid with cooper, silver, or gold. God was giving Moses the blueprint, if you will, to build a replica of the one that that was in heaven. Exodus 25:40, *"Look that thou make them after their pattern, which was shewed thee in the mount"* (also Heb. 8:5). Why was this so vital? Because the priesthood and the work of the High Priest was an illustration of something greater and more important to come afterward. Everything about the Tabernacle and the performance of the priesthood and High Priest was to be done exactly as instructed; the usual punishment for any violation was death. (Exo. 28:43; Num. 4:15, 20; 17:13; 2 Sam. 6:6, 7; Lev. 10:1, 2)

The substance of this shadow is Jesus, He is our High Priest! Therefore, (He) Jesus had to perform the same task in order to fulfill the ceremonial law. He (Jesus) had to take His own blood into the Holy of Holies in heaven and sprinkle it on the mercy seat for the atonement of sins for all the people; he could not be defiled before accomplishing the Atonement!

Bridging the Gap: A Journey from Law to Grace

Still not convinced, I've got another piece of evidence: Hebrews 9:11-14, 23-24: *"But Christ being come a High Priest of good things to come, by a greater and more perfect tabernacles, not made with hands, that is to say, not of this building; Neither by the blood of goats and calves, but by His own blood He entered in once into the Holy Place, having obtained eternal redemption for us. For if the blood of bulls and of goats, and the ashes of a heifer sprinkling the unclean, sanctifieth to the purifying of the flesh: How much more shall the blood of Christ, who through the eternal Spirit offered Himself without spot to God, purge your conscience from dead works to serve the living God"* ....

"It was therefore necessary that the pattern of things in Heaven should be purified with these; but the Heavenly things themselves with better sacrifices than these. For Christ is not entered into the Holy Place made with hands, which are the figures of the true, but into Heaven itself, now to appear in the presence of God for us."

If that don't light your fire, your wood is wet!

Now, that was complete, He could be touched without defilement!

SECTION 4

Grace: How NOW! Shall We Live?

Once the children of Israel were out of Egypt and on other side of the Red Sea, they fought and wandered for 40 years, yet, there was a land flowing with milk and honey, a land of promise, awaiting them.

That situation is a metaphor or shadow for our position on this side of the cross: though we are still battling our enemies, there is a city awaiting us where there will be no more crying, no pain, no sorrow but joy unspeakable joy for eternity.

But how shall we live this life? A life so meticulously planned by God, what assurances do we have to carry out God's purposes? Or, will we do like the children of Israel, murmur and complain at every turn?

For the children of Israel, the Law was given and written on tablets of stone, which they could not keep. In fact, within the 40 years of wandering all who left Egypt had died because of non-belief and faithlessness except Joshua and Caleb.

God has now, given us a new covenant and has written His Law on our hearts and because of the redemptive work of the Cross, Grace holds us within the bounds of the Law (II Cor. 3:3)………..and Christ's love (demonstrated by the blood He shed) covers a multitude of sin (I Peter 4:8 & I John 4:7).

Bridging the Gap: A Journey from Law to Grace

Under the law, if you broke one law you were guilty of breaking all the laws; under grace, we can receive forgiveness of our transgressions – it does not mean that we are guiltless; but it does mean we are blameless (Phil. 2:14-16).

Now! The just shall live by faith (Heb. 10:38).

Therefore, there is Now! No condemnation to those who are in Christ, who walk not after the flesh, but after the Spirit (Rom. 8:1).

But what does it mean to be – In Christ? To be in Christ or Christ in you is synonymous! Jesus said in John 14:10 *"I am in the Father and the father is in me…"*

But let's be clear, the Law given by Moses has been upgraded, if you will allow me to put it that way. Read Rom. 8:2-4 – *For what the law was powerless to do because it was weakened by the flesh,* (meaning WE could not keep it, my emphasis)*, God did by sending his own Son in the likeness of sinful flesh to be a sin offering. And so, he condemned sin in the flesh, in order that the righteous requirement of the law might be fully met in us, who do not live according to the flesh but according to the Spirit.* (NIV)

For the law of sin and death is now upgraded to the Law of the Spirit of Life, Adam vis-à-vis Jesus, Adam (man) to Jesus (Christ).

Again, I ask – "How NOW! Shall we live?" ……… By grace?

Grace according to Webster Dictionary:

1 – Unmerited help given to people by God

2 – Freedom from sin through divine grace

3 – A virtue coming from God

4 – A short prayer

5 – A temporary respite (as from the payment of a debt) and

6 – Ease of movement.

According to Strong's Concordance: all entries concerning grace in the Old Testament have the same meaning –

- 2580: kindness, favor. From the prime root 2603: to bend or stoop in kindness to one who is inferior; to move in favor of.

All entries in the New Testament concerning grace also have the same meaning –

- *5485*: a manner or act of divine influence upon the heart and its reflection in the life; including acceptable, benefit, favor, and gift. From the prime root *5463*: a verb meaning to be cheerful, happy or well off; Also implied in salutations such as greetings and farewells like "be well" and "God speed".

As we can see, the word grace has not and does not change in general meaning from Old to New Testament. It is kindness and favor unmerited, it's granting not what is required but what is desired by the giver; and oft-time offering up what is undeserved.

There have been many books written and sermons preached on the merits of Gods favor: building on the concept that "favor ain't fair". That is an absolutely correct statement of facts: to have favor on someone is to give special treatment to; to favor something is to reject something else. Therefore, favor (grace) is NOT fair! Therefore, everyone may not receive it to the same degree as another, at any given time.

Bridging the Gap: A Journey from Law to Grace

So, who are the candidates of this grace from God? What determines how much grace one receives? Are there some who are not given grace? NO! There is no one, born of a woman, who has not experienced God's grace. Titus 2:11 says, *"For the grace of God that bringeth salvation hath appeared to all men…"* Grace had run out for the people of Noah's generation. (Gen. 6:8) says, *"<u>But</u> Noah found grace in the eyes of the Lord."* I'm not saying God only has so much grace to give – but we all have an appointed time, (some even speed up their time by wasting it), but when that time arrives, grace for this life; whether perceived or unperceived, has ran out.

Grace was given under the old covenant but grace is lived through Jesus Christ (the new covenant) – John 1:17, *"For the law was given by Moses, but grace and truth came by Jesus Christ."*

How NOW! Shall we live?

BY GRACE and that through the message and teachings of Christ! For years the church has been preaching and teaching a message ABOUT Christ but not the message Christ taught! Now, I'm not saying a message about Christ is wrong. Everything about Christ, His life, and how he did what He did, is teachable and worth study – but are we hearing the Message He spoke?

Christ had a mission and a message that was singular: THE KINGDOM OF HEAVEN IS AT HAND! Everything Christ did after that, whether it was healing the sick, making the lame to walk, giving sight to the blind, or raising the dead, it was all to show and substantiate the Kingdom of God was at hand. Meaning it's near; it's here; it's before you… you're looking at it!

Bridging the Gap: A Journey from Law to Grace

He's mission was to re-store the Kingdom of God in the EARTH and on the earth. Now to restore the Kingdom of God on the earth God has to first and foremost restore it in the EARTH (mankind), Listen, mankind was formed from the dust of the ground, therefore EARTH! And God gave mankind dominion of that which he came from (earth); therefore, everything God does on the earth He has to do through the EARTH (mankind); therefore, to restore the Kingdom of God on the earth literally is a task for mankind to carry out; but God must first get the Kingdom in the EARTH (mankind). Selah.

Wherefore, Christ came to earth as a man, thereby giving Him authority: to impart to mankind, the manifested Glory (Holy Spirit) of the Kingdom of God; and to bestow to mankind the keys (assess) to the Kingdom of God; to discover the treasure that dwells therein. Now the mantel is passed and the perpetual restoration the Kingdom of God in the Earth is a task for mankind to carry out on the earth: reduplicating, replacing, repairing, replenishing, reinstating, re-surging, resurrecting, reviving, revealing, restoring, resourcing, resolving, regenerating, etc… all those things concerning God's perfect will for mankind that was lost by Adam (Rom. 12:2).

You notice the words used above referencing the purpose of Christ in relation to the Kingdom of God all start with the prefix (re). The prefix (re) indicates this is not the first time, but something is being done again or anew.

The truth of the matter is that Adam was given what we are striving for and what we are trying to achieve in our relationship with Christ! Adam walked in the fullness of the Holy Spirit. I say that based on what I read in the scriptures. Gen. 2:19 says *"And out of the ground the Lord God formed every beast of the field, and every fowl of the air; and brought them to Adam to see*

Bridging the Gap: A Journey from Law to Grace

what he would call them: and whatsoever Adam called every living creature, that was the name thereof."

Now what this says to us is that Adam had more power and ability than he knew he had. If I may paraphrase – God brought the animals (opportunity) to Adam to draw out the potential that He (God) placed there – Adam did not know he could do this! Where did this knowledge come from? I submit to you it came from the Holy Spirit that dwelt within him. Adam did not know what he possessed! Adam (mankind) was made in God's image and after His own likeness and carried the Spirit of God for he was a pure vessel without sin. But…. Once he (Adam) disobeyed (sinned) the Spirit of God could not continue to dwell in him – that's why God said "you shall surly die"; for without the Holy Spirit man is just a 'dead man walking' and a creature not fit for the Kingdom of God.

This scripture (Gen. 2:19), has even more riches for us! I am mindful of Malachi 3:6 that says, *"For I am the LORD, I change not ……"* Understanding, that, we too, like Adam, are made in God's image and do not realize the power and potential we possess; today, God still brings us opportunities to draw out the potential he has placed in us. But here's the key: whatever we call it …... that's what it will be!

Let's back up and look at Christ's message a bit closer. Matthew chapters 3 & 4 records Jesus being baptized by John and then led into the wilderness to be tempted by Satan. When he emerged Matt. 4:17 records His first sermon of rebuilding the Kingdom of God – *"Repent: for the Kingdom of Heaven is at hand"*. And again, in Mark 1: 15, *"The time is fulfilled, and the Kingdom of God is at hand: repent and believe the gospel"*. And again, in Luke 4:43, *"I must preach the Kingdom of God to other cities also: for therefore I am sent"*. That's His message, His mission, His purpose – and the task of restoring the Kingdom of God began!

What is this Kingdom of God? Where is the Kingdom of God? Is it a place we go to after death to be with Jesus as some has led us to believe? Or does AT HAND means here and NOW? I believe it means HERE and NOW! In Luke 17:20 & 21, the Pharisees demanded Jesus to tell them when the Kingdom of God shall come and Jesus responded, *"The Kingdom of God cometh not with observation; Neither shall they say look here! Or look there! For behold the Kingdom of God is within you"*. This is a strange saying! So here we have another shadow or metaphor to unravel.

KINGDOM DOMAIN PRINCIPAL

Let's see if I can explain this to you the way God has given it to me: A King must have territory in order to rule, do you agree? Although, **"A King Without a Country"** sounds like a good title for a movie!

Once a King steps into His territory and starts to exact His will in that territory, the territory now becomes His *Domain*. Your domain is your dwelling – like your house, your place of residence, where you live, and where your stuff is amen? Well. What we have now is a King in a domain – a King in domain – a King's domain – a Kingdom!

In essence, a Kingdom is a King in His Domain! What does that mean? You are made from dirt, which in essence is land or territory. When you allow King Jesus to come in and exact is will and purposes in you, you become His Domain and the Kingdom of God NOW dwells in you. Selah.

To understand "How NOW! Shall we live?" we must relate to Kingdom living!

KINGDOM LORDSHIP PRINCIPAL

It's His grace that allows us to live in the Kingdom of God! We are in the Kingdom at His pleasure and the Kingdom is in us by His invitation. Let's clarify something about Kingdom living, in this 21st century, we live in a democracy where we have individual rights (which motivates much of our self-centeredness). We call Jesus LORD but have no concept or model in our society by which to relate LORD-ship, except one, and that is the title LANDLORD!

We all understand that the landlord of a dwelling is the owner of the dwelling. You can only live there as long as you abide by the landlord's rules. You cannot knock down walls; add on to the building; dig holes in the yard, etc. without prior authority from the landlord. In fact, you must maintain the property to a satisfactory condition and pay the agreed upon monthly rent in order to live there. So, when we say Jesus is LORD of our lives – are we living that way? Or have we breached our contract? When we declare Him LORD, we declare Him owner of our lives! We cannot start renovating our lives; going in every which direction we choose; giving our life and hearts to others because they have a flashy smile and nice body; doing whatever feels good at the moment. There is a purpose and a plan that the LORD desires for your life. So, if He is not the owner of your life stop calling Him LORD, because if you call Him LORD but not live as though He's LORD, you are like a trespasser, and a squatter, who has not met the conditions to maintain that space. But the Word says in Philippians 2:10-11 that one day *"...every knee shall bow ...and every tongue shall confess that Jesus is LORD ..."*

I know that might sound a bit harsh and cold! It's not my intentions to offend you but Jesus said you shall know the truth and the truth will make you free. I'm just trying to put it in terms we can understand because in the Kingdom you do not have rights; you have promises: it's not a democracy.

KINGDOM PRINCIPAL OF KINGS

In the Kingdom, the Word of the King is sure; the decree of the King is law! We dwell there at His good pleasure; everything in the Kingdom belongs to the King – you own nothing! You are a steward. It is at the Kings pleasure to move His resources where He pleases to accomplish His purposes. Some unique qualities about a King:

- A king is never voted in or out of power

- a Kings authority is by birthright

- A King's Word is law

- A King personally owns everything in His domain

- A decree of a King is unchanging

- The King chooses who will be a citizen of His Kingdom

- The King embodies the government of His Kingdom's

- The King measures His wealth by the value of His property; and

- The Name of the King is the essence of His power.

KINGDOM COMMONWEALTH PRINCIPAL

In fact, the King's reputation is based on the welfare of the Kingdom's inhabitants. Who would want to live in a place where there are not adequate provisions? Who would want to live where the sun never shines and there is a cloud of doom and gloom hanging overhead? Where vultures linger and vipers lurk?

The Kingdom of God promises our need will be met! His is a Kingdom where the sun (Son) shines every day; He promised we can pick up vipers without fear, for He has not given us a spirit of fear; He made the flowers to grow and they are a sweet savory for our pleasure. He made waters to flow for our thirst; and planted trees for our nourishment. Yes, and He gives us the power to get wealth – but not to hoard it for our own selfish desires. When God gives more than you need, He trusts you to be an instrument to fulfill His purpose of blessing someone else. When you get abundantly blessed with more than you require, do you ask why? Or do you say "God is blessing ME!" and you proceed to shower <u>yourself</u> with "your blessing". Remember the parable of the rich fool (Lk. 12:16-20) who laid up treasure for himself, vs 21 says "…he that layeth up treasure for himself is not rich toward God"

KINGDOM ECONOMIC PRINCIPAL

Jesus told the rich ruler in Luke 18:22, "You still lack one thing. Sell everything you have and give it to the poor. And you will have treasure in heaven…

Bridging the Gap: A Journey from Law to Grace

For those of you who are prosperity worshipers, let me say this – and this is MY perception based on MY understanding of the word – The gospel of prosperity is NOT A KINGDOM MESSAGE! Prosperity, as it is defined, bantered and "gospelled" around is not the message of Jesus the Christ. The prosperity gospel says this: This is what God has blessed ME with! This is the ministry God spoke to ME and no one knows what I have endured to acquire this. But wait, God is no respective person! You just hold on! What He has done for me He will do for you! All the while they are saying this, they are asking you to continually give into their ministry to receive YOUR blessing, YOUR breakthrough, and YOUR deliverance! But what they are really saying is "this is mine, you got to get your own" because **they are not sharing the wealth**. They are living lavishly while most the congregation is struggling. My dear brothers and sisters this is not what the Word teaches!

There is prosperity in the Kingdom! But it does not consist of selfish desires and personal gain.

KINGDOM PRINCIPAL OF WORSHIP

Worship is an expression of "worthiness" or perceived value. The worship of the King is the citizens manifested expression of their gratitude and appreciation for the favor and privilege of being in His Kingdom. Worship involves giving back to the King a gift that indicates a true sacrifice from the giver. In the protocol of Kings, one never comes before a King without presenting a gift of great reward.

How do you please one who has everything? You honor them with accolades of their wisdom and generosity; with exaltations of their abilities and victories; while expressing one's dependency, which actifies the King obligation to care for His citizens who proclaim Him as

Bridging the Gap: A Journey from Law to Grace

their King. Exodus 23:25-26, *Worship the Lord your God, and his blessings will be on your food and water. I will take away sickness from among you, and none will miscarry or be barren in your land. I will give you a full life span.* (NIV)

So, worship of the King or giving to the King benefits the citizen more than it does the King; because everything already belongs to the King the citizen acknowledges his gratefulness; and it motivates the King to prove (with favor) he is greater than any other who might wish to be King.

I am reminded of a scripture, Matthew 2:11

And when they were come into the house, they saw the young child with Mary His mother, and fell down, and worshipped Him: and when (then) they opened their treasures, they presented unto Him gifts; gold, and frankincense, and myrrh.

Now, 2 Corinthians 4:7 tells us *"... we have treasure in this earthen vessel ..."* I believe, it's not until we truly worship the Lord that the gifts (treasures) we possess, can be open to present to Him (to whom it all belongs) and to use in His ministry.

These are just some of the principals we must govern our lives by. You can read more about Kingdom Principals in *"Kingdom Principals"* and *"Rediscovering the Kingdom"* by Dr. Myles Munroe, by which I excerpted these Kingdom Principals.

****

On the other hand, this journey; this walk in the way; (Jesus said "I am the way") this lifestyle is not easy! It's the greatest balancing act on earth! The Bible tells us that we are in the world but not of the world; also, that this is not our home but we are sojourners in a strange land. And, did not Jesus warn the disciple on several occasions and in many ways: that to follow Him would cost! I know there were times when Jesus' words sounded strange to the disciples. Statements like: *deny yourself and take up your cross and follow me* (Matt. 16:24); *he who put his hand to the plow and looks back is not fit for the Kingdom* (Lk 6:62); *they hated me and they will hate you also* (Jn. 15:18); *he who does not hate his mother, father, wife, sister, brother and even his own life, cannot be my disciple* (Lk. 14:26). These were hard, harsh and emphatic words signifying that choosing to follow would be costly! Not in a monetary way but in a more personal way: because He came to bring right relationship for mankind back to God, thereby restoring him back to a dominion man. Man took dominion over the physical earth but was never able to dominate the "earth" (himself), without the assistance of the Holy Spirit.

****

Many believers of that time believed Jesus would return in their lifetime; just as many do today, and have believed in every generation. Now, He may come in our generation and/or he may not. He prophesied things that will happen before His coming but He said *"...of that day and hour no man knows, no, not the angels of heaven, but my Father only"* (Matt. 24:36). But what was given to us to understand is the season on which His return is appointed (Rosh HaShanah); but that is a journey for another time.

My point being, believers throughout history have had a mistaken view of what was soon to come in their commitment to follow Christ. The Apostles had expectations of seeing an immediate inauguration of the Kingdom. Remember, just before His crucifixion, they argued about who would sit on His right hand and who would be the greatest among them in the Kingdom. It was as if they espoused to what we call today a "prosperity gospel". This is not what Jesus taught, but it was what they extracted from His words just as believers do today.

Bridging the Gap: A Journey from Law to Grace

The Apostles soon realized instead of peace and prosperity; suffering and persecution lay ahead for all the disciples. Jesus told us hard time was coming. We must no longer live out our lives with "favor, favor, favor" as a mindset. In light of world events, we must rethink our ministries; we must start to think not only offensively, but defensively as well. After being sifted as wheat, Peter said, *"Wherefore gird up the loins of our mind, be sober, and hope to the end for the grace that is to be brought unto you at the revelation of Jesus Christ"* (I Peter 113). In other words - purpose to be Holy in a godless world.

Jesus said in Matt. 11:12, *"From the days of John the Baptist until NOW, the Kingdom of heaven suffereth violence and the violent take it by force"*.

That word NOW is perpetual, the violence has not stop pressing against the Kingdom of God. When Jesus spoke of the Church He was building, He said "… the gates of hell will not prevail against it". Brothers and sister, we are the Church He is building, not one made with brick and mortar constructed by man. The forces of hell are pressing against us at every side while we are dancing around declaring "favor, favor, favor", naming and claiming things that don't belong to us. Favor is not something you lay hold to; it's not a birthright. God said," *...I will be gracious to whom I will be gracious, and will show mercy to whom I will show mercy"* (Ex. 33:19).

It's true, we, here in these United States, have enjoyed a "highly favored" status from a world view. But we are not the America that once acknowledged God within the moral fiber of how we governed our lives. Oh! We still "acknowledge" Him with our mouths, but obedience has become an "option" The Supreme Court and tolerance has become the moral thermometer: e.g. the abortion issues; same sex marriages; and divorces has become the norm. We have been

Bridging the Gap: A Journey from Law to Grace

in a bubble in our "normalcy", while many fellow Christians around the world are been martyred in the name of Jesus. The Word tells us plainly and unequivocally that suffering and persecution would not be estranged to us.

My personal opinion is that we have not, even with the help of the Holy Spirit, begun to live in the Kingdom of God! We need to stop living for grace: looking and expecting favor of the Lord; and start living intentional: by GRACE! When we start to live by GRACE, we will truly seek His face, truly humbling ourselves, understanding His heart, putting on the mind of Christ, seeing the world as God sees it – lost and we are God's answer. Without the facades, without the egos, without the big "I's" and little "you's', without being self-centered in ministry, showing Agape love (1 Cor. 13:1) toward those of the Household of Faith (John 13:35) and to others also.

"Sorrowful, yet always rejoicing; poor, yet making many rich; having nothing, and yet possessing everything (2 Cor.6:10). Jesus is your best friend as well as your King. Take His hand and walk-through life. Whatever you face: adventures, hardships, disappointments or pleasures, all will be experienced in the Spirit. He will create beauty out of ashes, peace out of chaos, joy out of sorrow. His friendship is real, yet clothed in manifested Glory. Living in His presence means living in two realms; the visible realm and the unseen realm. Here's a Kingdom Nugget: ***God's original purpose and intent was to rule the seen from the unseen through the unseen living in the seen on the scene.***

When we begin to appropriate God's GRACE
When we start to live by GRACE, we can see GRACE through the eyes of God rather than through natural eyes. God does not tailor GRACE to individuals, but has already custom-made GRACE to reflect

and reveal Christ. God uses GRACE to enlighten, illuminate, and awaken mankind to the WAY – to salvation.

SECTION 5

CONCLUSION

Let me come full circle: If sacrifices, circumcision, tithing, and Sabbaths were before the "Law", how are we to deal with them on this side of the cross, called "Grace"?

Tithing: It's true, Jesus did not teach specifically on tithing but He did speak much on giving and our attitude toward giving. In Luke 21:1-4 is the story of the widow who gives two mites into the offering. Jesus said while everyone is giving out of their abundance, this widow has giving more than all, because she gave all she had. She gave out of her poverty. Was it a tithe? Of all the snares and questions the Pharisees asked Jesus, they never questioned Him about tithing!!! Jesus and His disciples had money because Judas was the treasurer, and the only reason you need a treasurer is that you have excess funds. Yet, there's no mention of them tithing.

Paul didn't preach or write any letters on tithing. He did commend Philippians 4:15-19 on their willingness to give to the ministry; and Paul also asked of the Corinthians that donations be gathered before he got there: 2 Corinthians 9:6-7 *"But this **I** say* (Paul prefaced this as his own words, not thus said the LORD), *He which soweth sparingly shall reap sparingly; and he who soweth bountifully shall reap also bountifully. Every man according as he has purposed in his heart, so let him give; not grudgingly, or of necessity: for God loves a cheerful giver."*

Here, Paul is saying don't give out of necessity! In other words, because you feel you have to, or required to. Tithing was a moral law (Malachi 3:10), the tithe was for the priest, the

Bridging the Gap: A Journey from Law to Grace

priest could not own anything neither were they allowed to work. Numbers 18:20 says *"And the LORD spake unto Aaron, Thou shalt have no inheritance in their land, neither shalt thou have thy part among them: I am thy part and thine inheritance among the children of Israel."*

Aren't we, who are called by His name, not all priests?! Peter 2:9, we are referred to as a royal priesthood, yet we all don't receive tithes. I'm not advocating not giving tithes, but in the 20th century church, we have made tithing a doctrine and a millstone around the neck. Some have left the church feeling they are not worthy because they have not managed their finances to extract a tithe, therefore reimbursement and feelings of rejection have been presented giving the enemy, Satan, a place for condemnation.

In the concept of tithing: tithing isn't just about money! You can tithe your money; you can tithe your time; and you can tithe your talent. In fact, those whom have much pay their tithe religiously and proudly feel as though they have done their duty but rarely do anymore to help others. Matthew 23:23 says, *"Woe unto you, scribes and Pharisees, hypocrites! For ye pay tithe of mint and cummin, and have omitted the weightier matters of the law, judgment, mercy, and faith: these ought ye to have done, and not to leave the other undone."*

Now, was Jesus speaking to the Pharisees only or was He making an example for all His followers? Both! Jesus is saying anyone who pay tithes out of your substance (under the law) but leave out the other matters is a hypocrite. But here is what I heard… the weightier things are not the tithe!

Again, I am not advocating not giving tithe, but what I am saying is in your giving, if you designate it as tithe (10% of your earnings) or an offering; you do well, whether you give more or less; the important thing is to not give grudgingly or out of obligation but decide in your heart what you're going to give and do it cheerfully – for God loves a cheerful giver. And don't forget the weightier things also.

Circumcision: 1 Corinthians 7:18-20, *"Is any man called being circumcision? Let him not become uncircumcised. Is any man called uncircumcised? Let him not become circumcised. Circumcision is nothing, and uncircumcision is nothing, but the keeping of the commandments of God. Let every man abide in the same calling wherein he was called"*. As mentioned earlier, the cross) (this is my emphasis). And as it abolished the animal sacrifice it also eliminated the work of the High priest because everyone now has access to the Holy of Holies, but mind you it does not eliminate HOW we approach the Throne of Grace.

I must make mention here on a purpose of God that did not have a shadow to foretell, because He is Sovereign: the institution of sacrifices from times of old were well established, but never did a sacrificed lamb EVER come back to life! The giving of His life satisfied salvation – so why did he rise again to life?

When Jesus said "IT IS FINISHED!" Many have preached that all was done, what he came to do was complete. If this was the case there was no need for the resurrection. So, what was finished? The DEBT! The debt owed by sin. Jesus paid the bill (1 Cor. 6:20). The sin debt was paid by His death. The promise made to Adam, that he would die, therefore, we all die without redemption. Jesus paid the debt with His blood, laying down His life as a sacrifice for redemption of all mankind.

Christ's work continued in His resurrection! Leading the way for all believers of all time to follow his lead. 1 Cor. 15:20 & 23 says, *"But now is Christ risen from the dead, and become*

Bridging the Gap: A Journey from Law to Grace

the first fruit of them that slept." Vs23 *"Every man in his own order: Christ the first fruit; afterwards they who are Christ's at His coming."*

Then He had to complete the work of the High Priest in the Holy of Holies in Heaven! Which we have already discussed.

My conclusion is this: He rose because He could not reign and rule over a Kingdom from the grave! He had to be a living, viable, victorious King to reign over a Kingdom implemented from the foundation of the world. You will find many scriptures concerning His eternal rulership.

circumcision was a sign of the covenant, an act of obedience and compliance. We now have a new and better covenant, on this side of the cross; it's a covenant of grace; bought, purchased, contained, sealed, and signed in the blood of Jesus.

Moreover, the circumcision we are to desire is the circumcision of the heart. Romans 2:28, *"For a person is not a Hebrew who is one outwardly, and true circumcision is not something visible in the flesh. On the contrary, a person is a Hebrew who is one inwardly, and circumcision is of the heart – by the Spirit…"*

Sacrifices: Malachi 3:6 says, *"For I am the LORD, I change not…."* God has not changed His mind or the pathway to Him; only now, we don't bring animals to a High priest, but we bring ourselves: as a living sacrifice. Romans 12:1 says, *"… that ye present your bodies a living sacrifice, holy, acceptable unto God……"*

When Jesus died on the cross, at the exact moment, the veil in the temple was rent; torn from the top to the bottom, signifying (I don't need this sacrifice anymore, my sacrifice is on the

Sabbaths: Colossians 2:14 says, *"Blotting out the handwriting of ordinances that was against us* (Law), *which was contrary to us, and took it out of the way, nailing it to the cross;*

Bridging the Gap: A Journey from Law to Grace

and having spoiled principalities and powers, He made a show of them openly, triumphing over them in it. Let no man therefore judge you in meat, or drink, or in respect of a Holyday, or of the new moon, of the Sabbath Days: which are a shadow of things to come; but the body is of Christ.

Sabbaths Days are a shadow of things to come: a shadow is only a silhouette; it cannot be harmed neither can it do any harm. It is only an image of something else! Yet, you cannot see details or important characteristics of the subject matter. But …. If you follow the shadow… it will lead to the substance of which it is casted.

Each and every Feast Day / Holy Day, God established with the Israelites was first viewed as a High Sabbath, which distinguished it from the weekly Sabbath and required detailed adherence to keep it as God commanded: whence the shadow is cast and the ground work laid for the Messiah, which is Jesus.

I would be remiss if I did not point you to Hebrews 4th Chapter, where the Sabbath is interpreted in three different ways: 1 as the literal weekly rest; 2 as the rest that can be assured by faith in Jesus; and 3 as the seventh day yet to come, a prophetic day.

1. *Let us therefore fear, lest, a promise being left us of entering into His rest, any of you should seem to come short of it;* This is the command and the promise of supply God gave the Israelites in the wilderness – to remember the Sabbath and keep it Holy!

2. *For we which have believes do enter into His rest;* This is the promise of Jesus when He said "…*come to me all ye who are heavy laden and I will give you rest."*

3. *Today if ye will hear His voice, harden not your hearts. For if Jesus had given them rest, then He would not afterward have spoken of another day. There remaineth*

therefore a rest to the people of God. This is the promised rest of dwelling with him in eternity.

Here is revelation God gave me while writing this: That the "rest" of the LORD is a sucker punch to Satan. Satan had no idea that man would eventually live forever, even though he (Satan) made him (mankind) to disobey God's directive; Satan believed God when He said to man, that mankind would die the day they ate from the forbidden tree. So the fact that Jesus rose to life as a first fruit of those who followed Him, nullified everything Satan set in motion; and not only gave Jesus victory over sin but exalts resurrected mankind to judge angels (1 Cor. 6:3), of which he himself (Satan) is a fallen angel.

I've attempted to expose the shadow of this Holy Day called Passover, in an effort to lead you to its substance, Christ the anointed one. As with all 7 Holy Days, the shadow casted is that of the Anointed One, Christ manifested mission intervening into the lives and affairs of mankind.

So.... How do we balance this life we are to live out in this mortal body? I Peter 4: 12-13, *"Beloved, think it not strange concerning the fiery trial which is to try you, as though some strange thing has happened unto you. But rejoice, inasmuch as ye are partakers of Christ's sufferings; that, when His glory shall be revealed, ye may be glad also with exceeding joy".*

Therefore, I challenge you to embrace and accept the invitation of the King to enter into His Kingdom. Renew your citizenship by accepting the redemptive sacrifice made by King Jesus Himself. Open your gates and allow the King to exact His will in your life thereby transforming your territory into His domain and establishing the Kingdom of God within you. I am not prompting you to join a religion or to engage in meaningless rituals but to depart from denominational tenants (traditions) for there is but one body, and embrace the Kingdom of God, the teachings of Jesus, as sons and daughters, renewing your rightful status as a citizen of the Kingdom of Heaven.

Blessings

Made in the USA
Monee, IL
24 October 2024